THE HOW AND WHY WONDER BOOK OF
BEGINNING
SCIENCE

By DR. JEROME J. NOTKIN, Science Supervisor,
Suffolk County, N. Y.
Professor, Hofstra College
and SIDNEY GULKIN, M. S. in Ed.,
Teacher, New York City

Illustrated by WILLIAM FRACCIO
and TONY TALLARICO

Editorial Production: DONALD D. WOLF

Edited under the supervision of

Dr. Paul E. Blackwood
Specialist for Elementary Science
U. S. Department of Health, Education
and Welfare, Washington, D. C.

Text and illustrations approved by

Oakes A. White
Brooklyn Children's Museum
Brooklyn, New York

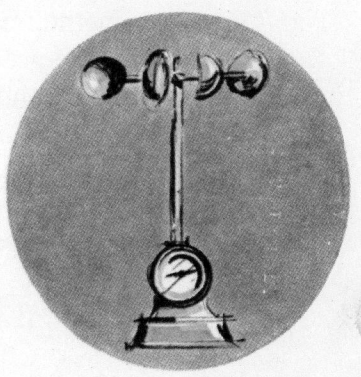

SCHOOL EDITION
Charles E. Merrill Books, Inc.
By special arrangement with Wonder Books, Inc.

Introduction

This book is another in a series of *How and Why Wonder Books* planned to open doors of scientific knowledge to young readers. A quick look into the book reveals that it deals with several important areas of science: light, weather, plants, machines, and electricity. This general approach will have a special appeal to readers who wish an overview of more than one area of science within a single book.

In addition, this book helps the reader himself become more scientific by emphasizing experiments as a way of making discoveries. Young investigators will be pleased to see that over two dozen experiments are suggested. All of them are easy to do and require only simple equipment. They can be done at home by parents and children together, or they can be done at school. In either event, children can have fun and, at the same time, learn a great deal about this basic method used by scientists.

Youngsters who are eager to learn will find this book of great help in exploring and understanding their environment, and they will want to add it to their shelf of *How and Why Wonder Books*.

Paul E. Blackwood
Specialist for Elementary Science
U. S. Department of Health, Education and Welfare
Washington, D.C.

Foreword

This is a book about basic ideas in science. You don't have to be a college student or even a high-school boy or girl to understand these ideas. Try to do some of the things suggested here, and you will begin to understand why science is so important in our lives. You will see for yourself how weather instruments work—how they help in predicting the weather. You will take a nail, some insulated wire, and a dry cell, and make it behave like a magnet whenever you want to, and then take its power away. Just like that.

No, this is not a book to teach you magic or tricks. It's even better. It's a book about old ideas that will remain new and always true. These ideas will help you make things now to have fun with, and later on will help you build bridges, invent new machines, and perhaps discover new ways to promote long life and good health.

Do as many of the projects as you can. If you don't succeed the first or second time, try again. You will have lots of fun trying.

Good luck!

Jerome J. Notkin
Sidney Gulkin

CONTENTS

Light in Our Lives

Important Words

Photon: A tiny bundle of light energy.

Reflection: Bouncing of light rays in straight lines.

Refraction: Bending of light rays as they go from one substance to another.

The tremendous gains made in the area of artificial lighting can be measured by the contrast shown above.

Have you ever heard someone say, "Turn the light on — I can't see a thing"? Or: "We'll have to wait until the sun rises before we can see"?

Without light we would be lost. A long time ago people depended upon the light of the sun to do their work. They would begin to work when the sun rose and would stop when the sun set.

Then people discovered fire and found that it could light rooms at night. You know the famous story about how Abe Lincoln used to read a great deal in front of his fireplace just to get the light from the fire. Of course, many people used candles, if they could afford them. Later a fuel—kerosene— was used in special lamps.

Still later, gas—illuminating gas— gave us light in our homes and even on our streets.

Finally electricity came along, so that we now have all the artificial light we need.

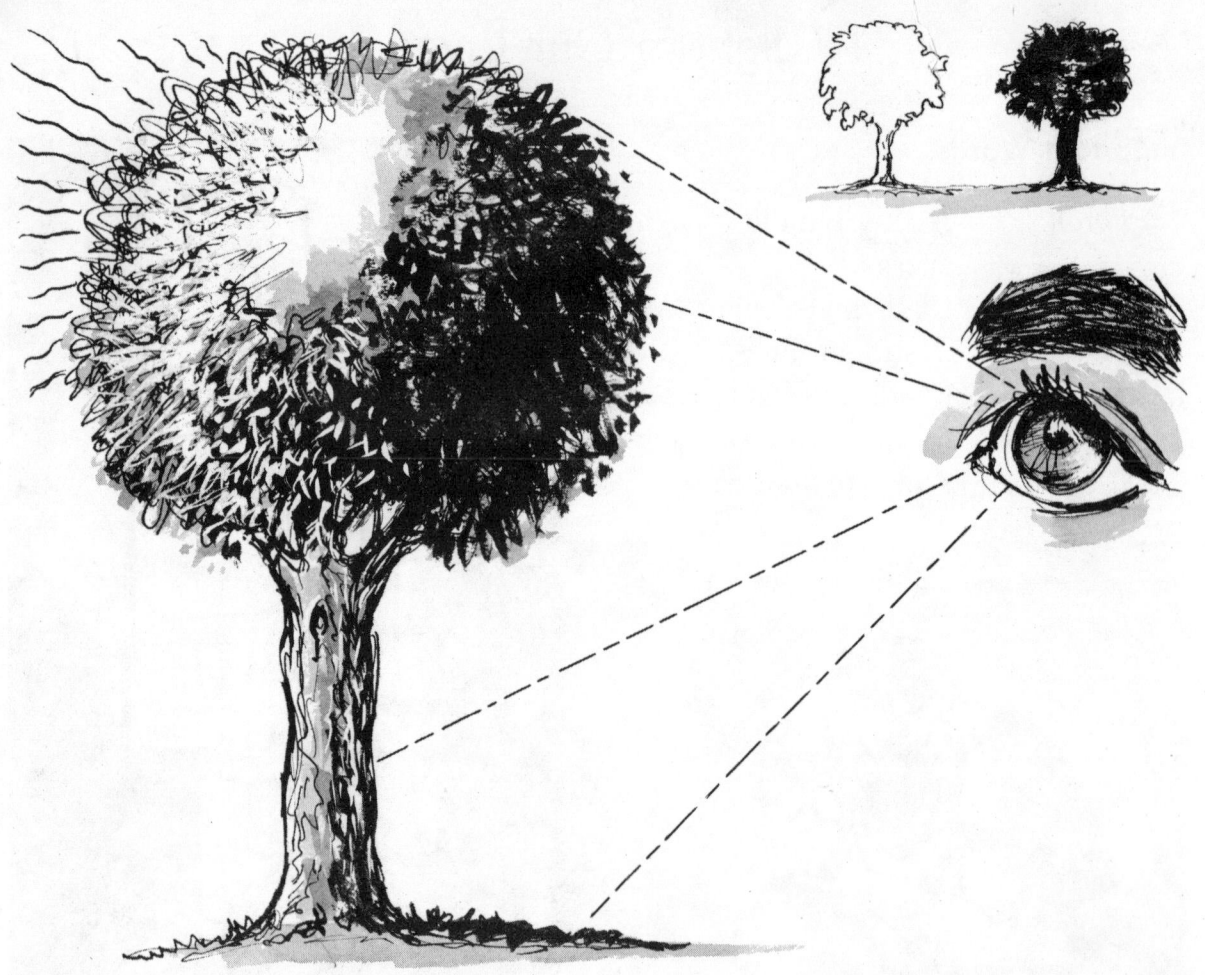

Light is wonderful. But what is it?

Let's see. Some of the greatest minds in the history of mankind have been asking and trying to answer the question: "What is light?"

Among the people who helped make great discoveries about light were such scientific giants as Sir Isaac Newton, James Clerk-Maxwell, and Max Planck. It is Planck's theory that tells us that light is a flow of bundles of energy. These bundles of energy are referred to as PHOTONS. This is, of course, a very simple attempt to explain a difficult theory. As we learn more science, we will learn a great deal more about light.

Scientists are funny people in a way. Once they find out one thing, they begin

When photons hit an object which absorbs them, the object looks dark. If the photons bounce back to your eye, the object reflects light. See diagram above.

wondering how to find out more. That is what happened to the great Danish scientist, Olaus Roemer. He figured that the speed of light was about 186,000 miles per second. He was fairly accurate. Mind you, this was in 1675. In our own times an American scientist, Albert Michelson, in a very difficult experiment found that light travels at 186,285 miles per second. As you can see, our friend Roemer came close to the accurate measurements Dr. Michelson made.

You can find out many interesting things about light and have fun at the same time.

How Can You Read Mirror Writing?

You will use:

Three mirrors about 4 by 4 inches
One shoebox without a cover
Cellophane tape
Front page of a newspaper
Scissors

Do this:

Stand one mirror up in a corner of the shoebox. Place a second mirror alongside it, so that both mirrors touch in one corner of the box at right angles to each other.

Tape the mirrors in place.

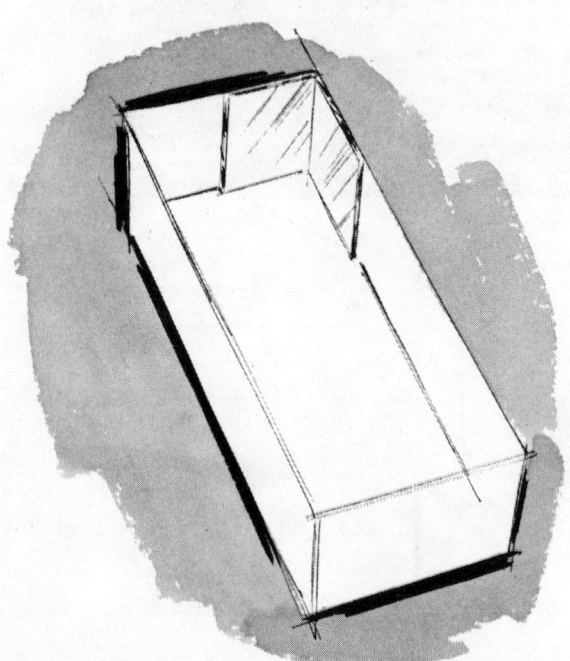

Preparing a box with mirrors to read mirror-writing

Cut out the corner of the box with the mirrors, cutting across the dotted line along the bottom of the box.

Now mount three or four words of a newspaper headline on a piece of cardboard. Our headline reads: "CITY IN DARKNESS."

Place it in front of the third mirror. Can you read it, or is it reversed?

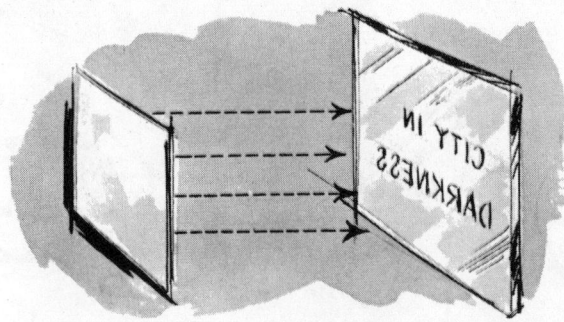

One of the corner mirrors reverses the writing.

Now place the headline in front of your corner mirrors. Look right into the corner between the mirrors. Is the writing reversed, or can you read it?

It should read: "CITY IN DARKNESS."

Why does it work?

What actually happened is that one of the corner mirrors reversed the writing, while the second mirror re-reversed it back to the normal order of writing we can read.

This is not a trick. It is a science experiment that any boy or girl can do. You will accomplish two things—learn an idea in science and have a lot of fun.

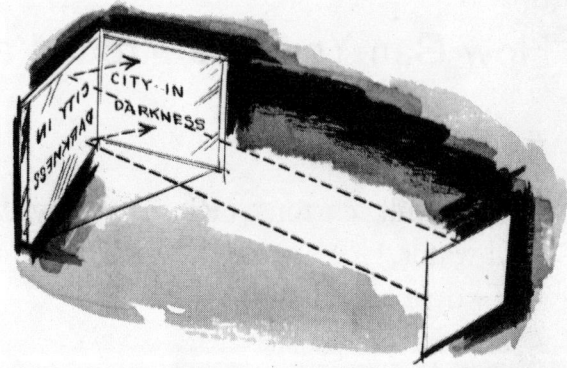

The second mirror re-reverses writing, now readable.

How Can You See Around a Corner?

You will use:

Two milk cartons (Rinse well with cold water.)
Two small mirrors
Adhesive tape
Knife

Do this:

Cut off the tops of both milk cartons.

Insert the open end of one carton into the open end of the other, so that they form a 16-inch tube.

One inch from the bottom of one of

the cartons, cut out a window in the side 1½ inches high.

Cut a slit in the same side, ½ inch from the bottom.

Insert a mirror, face up, in the slit until one end rests along the back of the carton. Secure the mirror with tape at the angle shown in the illustration.

Do the same thing with the opposite side of the other carton.

The reflecting sides of the mirrors should be facing each other.

You have made a periscope.

Try looking out the window by looking into the lower part of the periscope, while the upper part is above the window ledge. You can look out the window or around corners while you are out of sight.

The periscope which you can build yourself is based on the same principle as a real one found in a sub.

Why does it work?

The reason you can do all of these things is that light travels in a straight line. The mirrors reflect the rays of light.

Try reading through a periscope. Let someone hold a newspaper and see if you can read the headlines. Is it mirror writing? Can you explain it?

The reason you were able to read the headline in the periscope is because mirror A made mirror-writing which mirror B reversed to normal writing.

How Can You Bend Light?

You will use:

A large, clear drinking glass
Teaspoon

Do this:

Fill the glass with water.
Place a spoon in the glass.
Look at the spoon from many different positions. The spoon will appear to be broken.

Why does it work?

Light travels faster through air than it does through water. In passing in or out of water, light rays change their direction slightly.

This is called refraction. It occurs when light passes from air to a denser material such as water or glass, where its speed is slowed down.

The word "refraction" is often confused with "reflection."

That often happens, because many science words for different things sound alike. You can play a game—a science word game—with your friends. See if they can tell you the difference between sound-alike words.

The oar in the water (or a teaspoon in a glass) appears broken. It only seems so due to refraction of light.

The light "bounces" from the mirror to the ceiling.

How Can You Bounce Light?

You will use:

A small mirror

Do this:

Hold the mirror so that you catch some light right on it, and direct it to a wall or ceiling.

Move the mirror quickly. Move it slowly. Direct it to other parts of the room.

Why does it work?

Some rays of light landed on the mirror and bounced right off—that is, the light rays were reflected to the wall.

If you notice carefully, you will see that the rays reflect off the mirror at exactly the same slant, or angle, that they hit it. This shows us that light travels in straight lines.

We know from experience and scientific observation that white materials reflect the sun's rays, while darker or black materials absorb them. That is

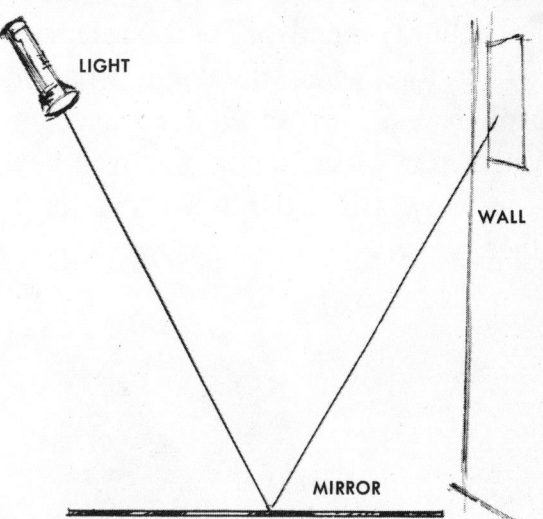

Rays reflect off mirror at the same angle they hit it.

why people living in warm climates wear white clothing. Do you remember pictures you have seen of Arabs in the desert? It is always cooler to wear a white shirt or dress in the summertime so that the sun's rays bounce off and away from you.

Can You See a Rainbow Other Than in the Sky?

You will use:

A prism or a triangular ornamental crystal from a chandelier

Do this:

Hold the prism in a path of sunlight so that light will pass somewhere through the center.

Don't be discouraged if a rainbow is not seen at once. Move the prism until you begin to see beautiful colors.

Why does it work?

When light travels from a lighter substance such as air to a heavier substance such as glass or water, it slows down. The light rays bend, or are refracted.

Therefore, when white light is passed through a prism, we can see its component parts—the colors of a rainbow —as they are separated from each other.

The prism breaks up bright light into its components.

How Can You Burn Paper Without a Match?

You will use:

Magnifying glass
Piece of paper
Metal pan
Water

Do this:

Place the paper in a metal pan as a safety precaution.

Try to catch some rays of the sun on your glass, and direct them onto the piece of paper.

Hold the glass long enough and the

How Can You Make a Rainbow Without a Prism?

You will use:

Pan with water
Mirror

Do this:

Place a mirror at an angle inside the water-filled pan.

Place the pan in the path of a strong source of light. The rays should strike the mirror in the water.

A rainbow should be on the wall.

Why does it work?

As light struck the mirror, it was reflected. However, it was also refracted, or bent, because the rays passed through more than one substance.

The bending light rays separated into their many parts, each one traveling at a different speed. The result was the rainbow colors on the wall.

paper will begin to smoke and catch fire.

Pour water into the pan. Be sure that the fire is completely out.

Why does it work?

When the rays of the sun struck the convex lens (that's the type of lens a magnifying glass has), they converged, or were refracted to one point. Remember that the sun gives light and heat. The heat was so concentrated that it ignited the paper.

Fire is not a toy to play with. A good scientist is a careful one. Be sure to do experiments involving fire in the presence of an adult.

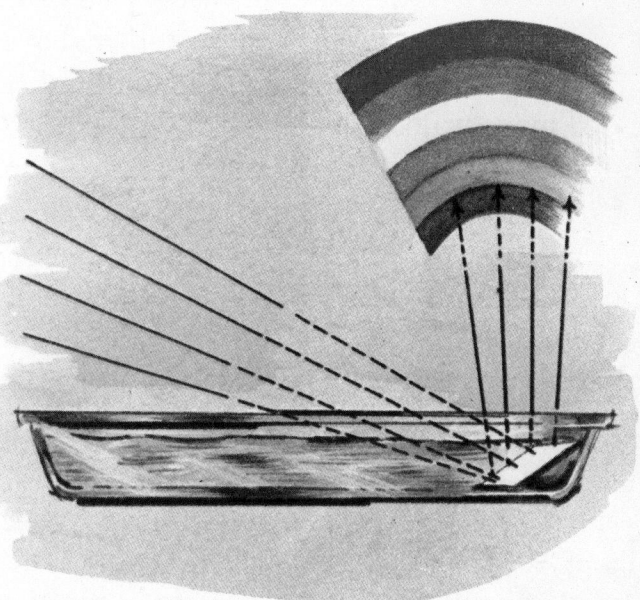

This light is reflected and refracted at the same time.

Electricity—Magic at Your Finger Tips

Important Words

Dry Cell: A combination of two different materials in a chemical solution which produces electricity.

Electron: Tiny particle that carries a minus charge of electricity.

Fuse: Acts as a policeman to warn us of danger. The fuse melts when too many electrons are flowing. This breaks the circuit.

Volt: Unit for measuring electrical pressure.

Watt: Unit for measuring electrical power.

We have been told that magic has no place in science. But if Michael Faraday could see some of the modern uses for electricity, he might say, "It *must* be magic!"

Just think how you used electricity today. Were you awakened by an electric alarm clock? Did your father shave with an electric razor? Did your mother make waffles on an electric waffle iron?

You may have watched television before going to school. If you rode a bicycle to school, you probably used the horn—electricity makes it work.

Were the lights on in your classroom? Did your principal speak to the school over the loudspeaker? Did you see a movie or a filmstrip in class?

Think of all the other things in the world that electricity makes work, and you will see why anyone might use the word "magic" for it.

A magic trick, however, cannot usually be repeated successfully at home. But many scientific experiments can be carried out by anyone. In fact, it isn't always necessary to have a great deal of equipment. Much of it can be homemade.

So let's forget the word "magic" and replace it with "understanding" and "knowledge."

When a scientist is puzzled by something, he tries to find the answer by doing several things. He observes whatever puzzles him very carefully. He then writes down what he sees. Then he studies this information to see if he can get an idea about it. He calls this idea a theory. Next, he goes about trying to prove whether or not the theory is correct.

Scientists have a theory about the

nature of electricity. To understand this theory, we must begin with another theory. This one deals with the "building blocks" of the universe.

Everything that you can think of is made up of molecules. If you take the smallest drop of water and divide it in half, and in half again, and again and again, you will be left with one invisible molecule. This is true of all things.

A molecule of water is made up of three smaller particles, called atoms. There are two atoms of hydrogen and one atom of oxygen.

Just as all of our words are made up of combinations of 26 letters, so all things in the world are made up of combinations of about 100 atoms. That is why we call atoms the "building blocks" of the universe.

Atoms, themselves, are composed of

In the year 1752, Benjamin Franklin, the famous American statesman and scientist, proved that lightning was a form of electricity. He attached a metal key to the cord of a kite and one day, during a thunderstorm, Franklin flew his kite. Whenever lightning hit the flying kite above, sparks flew from the key.

still smaller particles called electrons, protons, neutrons, and several others.

Scientists tell us that electricity is made up of the electrons that are part of all material. When we get these electrons to move, we have an electric current—electricity.

We make these electrons move—so

15

Hydroelectric plant: The great force of the falling water collected behind the dam activates the generator.

that they can work for us—in generators which may be far from our homes or factories.

Fuel such as coal or oil is used to make these generators turn and make the electrons flow. Often steam is used. Sometimes falling water from a dam turns fan-shaped wheels called turbines. A shaft is attached to each turbine. When that shaft turns inside a generator, or dynamo, electricity comes out.

The electricity—or moving electrons—is pushed through wires toward our homes, factories, farms, and wherever it is needed.

This push, or pressure, is measured in volts. The voltage in the wires along the way is very high, but when it comes into your house, it has been reduced to 110 to 220 volts.

Now it can be used to operate your television set, electric trains, toaster, vacuum cleaner, and many other appliances.

How did people light their homes and streets before Thomas Edison invented the electric light?

The cave men used torches.

The ancient Greeks and Romans had oil lamps to light their way.

The early settlers in this country used candles.

Later, a way was found to use gas for light and kerosene lamps.

But it wasn't until about eighty years ago that the first electric light was used. A light bulb is called an incandescent lamp. This means that the wire in the bulb is heated until it glows. Our sun is also incandescent.

Perhaps you are lucky enough to be in a new school. It is likely that your room is lighted by another type of lamp —a fluorescent lamp.

Fluorescent lamp: More light than incandescent ones.

People often ask, "What is the real difference between the incandescent lamp and the fluorescent lamp?"

The main difference is in the way they give off light. The incandescent filament, made of tungsten, is heated by the electricity flowing through it to such an extent that it glows white hot.

In the fluorescent lamp, moving electrons pass through the mercury gas that fills the tube. This produces ultraviolet rays which strike chemicals that coat the inside of the tube. The chemicals glow, and we have light.

We get more light and less heat with fluorescent lamps.

How Does an Incandescent Lamp Glow?

You will use:

Dry cell
Short piece of iron picture wire
Pliers

Do this:

Connect a short piece of iron picture wire to the two terminals of a dry cell. In a little while the wire will become warm and will glow.

Note: This reduces the life of the dry cell, so do not keep the wire connected for too long.

Caution: Disconnect the wire with a pair of pliers to avoid burning yourself.

Why it works:

The wire completes the circuit so that electrons can flow from one terminal of the dry cell to the other.

The electricity is changed into heat and light energy.

This is similar to the way an incandescent lamp works.

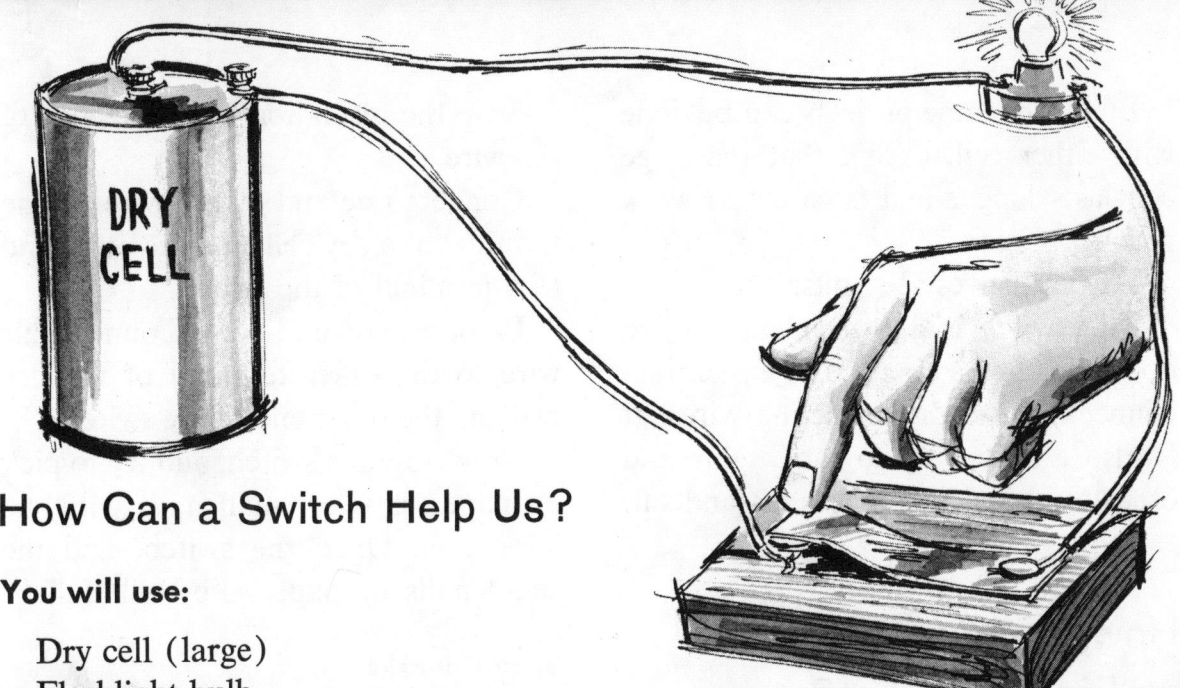

How Can a Switch Help Us?

You will use:

Dry cell (large)
Flashlight bulb
Miniature socket
Insulated copper wire
Piece of metal
Block of wood
Two nails
Hammer

Do this:

Take a piece of metal—4 inches long, 1 inch wide (you can cut it from a tin can if you are careful).

Nail one end of it on the block of wood.

Place another nail in the wood under the other end of the metal.

Do not place either nail all the way down in the wood.

Be sure that the loose end of the metal is not resting on the nail beneath it.

Now you have a switch.

With wires all in place, the circuit has been closed.

Connect one wire from either terminal of the dry cell to the nail under the metal.

Be sure to strip the insulation from the ends of all the wires you use.

Connect a second wire from the other terminal of the dry cell to either terminal of the miniature socket.

Connect a third wire from the other terminal of the socket to the nail holding the strip of metal in place.

Now press the switch.

If you have made all the connections right, the circuit now is closed, and the light will go on.

Save this switch. You will probably use it many times.

Why it works:

If you have a large dry cell, notice the two terminals at the top.

This makes connecting wires to it much easier than connecting them to a small flashlight cell.

But all of these projects can be done with either cell, except that the large cell lasts longer and is easier to work with.

Each cell gives 1½ volts.

The switch is a convenient way to open and close a circuit. It is easier than connecting and disconnecting wires. It is also a safer way to turn lights and other electrical appliances on and off.

How Can You Make an Electromagnet?

You will use:

Dry cell
Wire
Switch
Large nail
Small nails or paper clips

Do this:

Wind about ten turns of wire around a large nail.

Strip the insulation from the ends of the wire.

Connect one end of the wire to one terminal of a dry cell, and the other end to a terminal of the switch.

Prepare a second wire. Connect this wire to the other terminal of the dry cell and the other end of the switch.

Now close the switch, and try to pick up paper clips or small nails with the large nail. Open the switch, and the small nails or paper clips will fall.

Why it works:

The electricity from one part of the dry cell flows through the many turns of wire back into the dry cell.

When electricity flows through a wire, the wire has magnetic power around it. If the wire happens to be in the form of a coil, the magnetism is even stronger.

An iron nail inside the coil becomes a magnet. This is true only so long as the electricity is flowing in the circuit. It is a magnet when you want it to be.

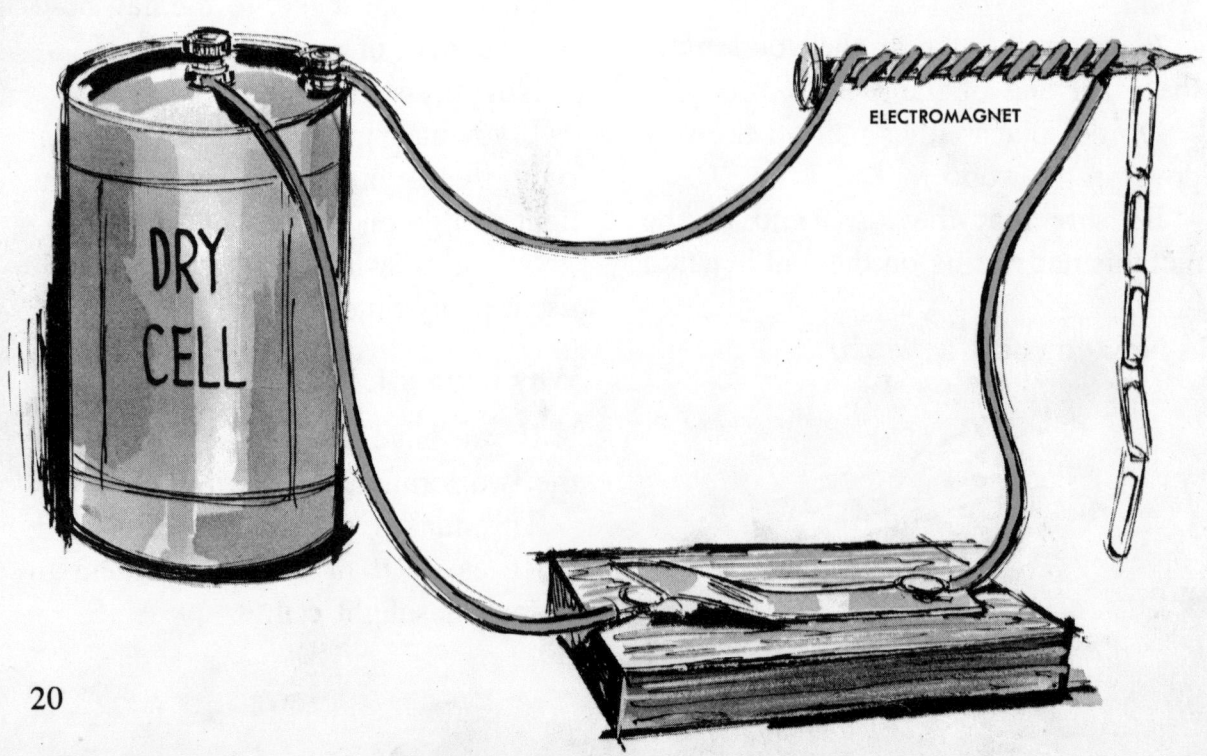
ELECTROMAGNET

DRY CELL

How Can You Make a Horseshoe Electromagnet?

You will use:

Thin bolt with nut
Insulated copper wire
Dry cell
Switch
Small nails or paper clips

Do this:

Place a long, thin bolt in a vise. Bend it into a U-shape. Wind several layers of wire around one arm of the U. Move across to the other arm and wind as shown in the diagram.

Strip the insulation from the ends of the wire.

Connect one end of a piece of wire to one terminal of the dry cell, and the other end to the terminal of the switch.

Connect a second piece of wire between the dry cell and the switch.

Close the switch. How many paper clips or nails can you pick up with your horseshoe electromagnet?

Open the switch. What happens? Try this several times.

Why it works:

We already know why an electromagnet works. (See previous experiment.)

What are the advantages of an electromagnet shaped like this?

We are now able to take advantage of the magnetism produced in both ends, or poles, of the electromagnet. When both poles are near each other, we get twice the strength that a straight bolt gives—if the number of turns of wire is the same on each side.

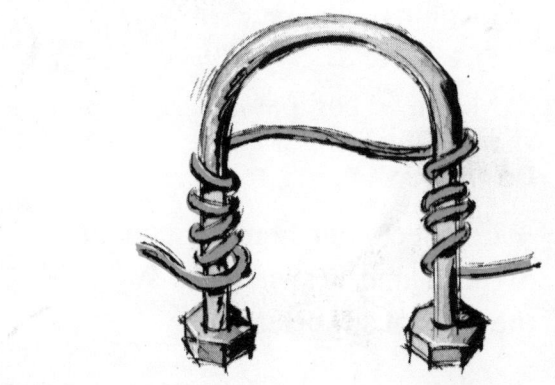

How to wind a bolt

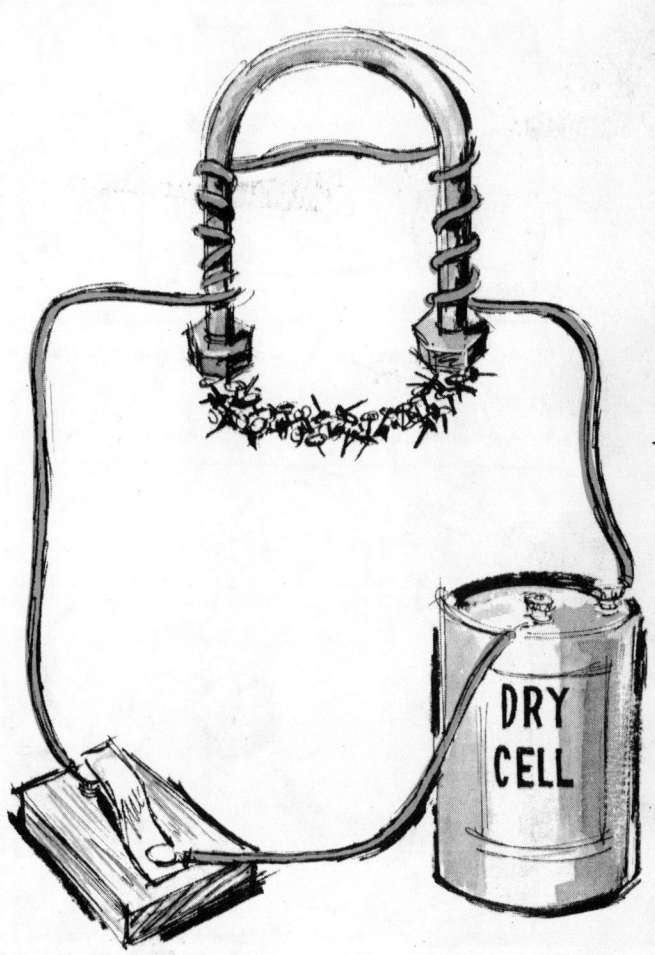

Horseshoe electromagnet will produce magnetism.

How Can You Test the Polarity of an Electromagnet?

You will use:

Electromagnets you have made
Switch
Insulated copper wire
Dry cell
Magnetic compass

Do this:

Connect your horseshoe magnet to a dry cell and a switch, as suggested in the previous experiment.

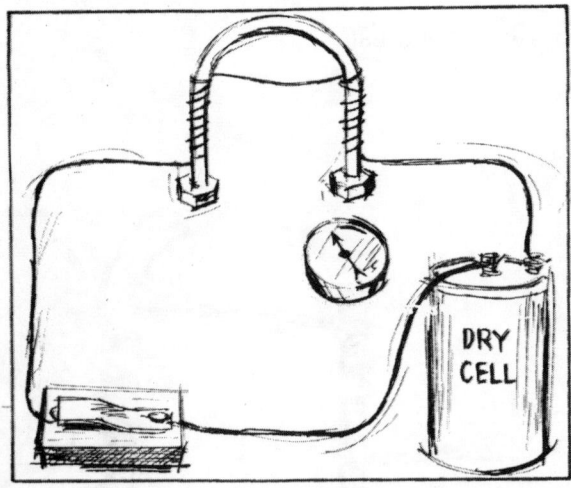

Place a compass as shown and close the switch.

Wires connected to the dry cell are now reversed.

Bring a magnetic compass near one of the poles of your electromagnet. Close the switch. What happens to the needle of the compass? Which pole of the compass was attracted to the pole of your electromagnet?

Move the compass near the other pole of the electromagnet. Close the switch again. What happens this time?

Why it works:

We know that the opposite poles of a magnet—that is, north and south—attract each other. Like poles—north and north, or south and south—repel each other. You can tell which pole is which by testing with a magnetic compass. Try to determine the polarity of your horseshoe electromagnet. Remember that the compass itself is a magnet.

What do you think would happen if you reversed the two wires connected to the dry cell? Try it and see how much fun you can have.

Do you see how magnetism and electricity are related?

Our magnet really depends on the electricity it gets from the dry cell.

We find electromagnets all around us. We find them in refrigerators, in television sets, in telephones, in Dad's electric shaver, and in Mother's vacuum cleaner.

Electricity can be your friend or your enemy. Don't try to argue with it. If you make a mistake, it will be too late to say, "I'm sorry." You can use electricity as a powerful and dependable servant if you learn some very important safety rules.

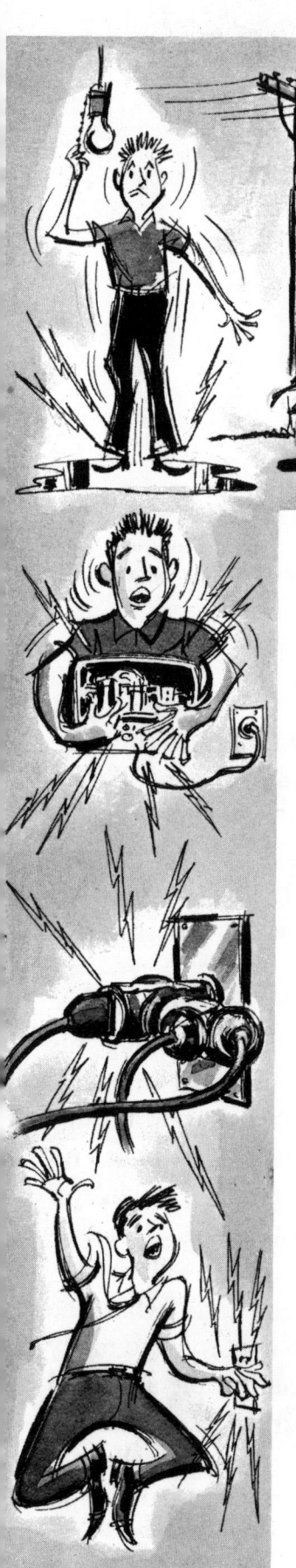

Safety Rules

Never touch a switch with wet or damp hands.

Never overload your connections.

Never poke around a radio or television set if the switch is on.

Never pull the chain of a light bulb if you are standing on a wet floor.

Never, never touch a broken cable after or during a storm, or even if the sun is shining. Call a policeman or a fireman.

Never touch an electrical appliance, switch, radio, or television set while bathing or when wet.

Never put electrical wires under carpets.

Never put a penny in the fuse box. Use a fuse of the proper size.

Never place anything except an electrical plug into a wall socket.

Never remain in a lake during a thunderstorm.

Never remain under or near a tree during an electrical storm or a thunderstorm. Find other shelter quickly.

Many people are interested in forecasts: sailors, farmers, pilots and even those going on a picnic.

Everybody Talks About the Weather

Important Words

Barometer: An instrument used to measure the pressure of the atmosphere.

Thermometer: An instrument used to measure temperature.

Meteorology: The science dealing with the study of weather.

Humidity: Moderate dampness.

Radiosonde: A radio device carried aloft by a balloon, which relays atmospheric pressure, temperature, and humidity.

What is the first thing you do after you wake up each morning? Do you try to get back under the covers for a few more minutes? Do you start to sing? Or do you do what many other people do —peer outdoors to see what kind of weather it is? This helps you decide what type of clothing to wear.

Many people are vitally interested in the weather.

Bad weather might prevent a fisherman or a farmer from earning his living. Think about it for a moment, and you will realize how important this is. Can you understand why pilots receive weather checks regularly while in the air? A skipper of a ship also needs to know what the weather will be like.

Knowing ahead of time what the weather will be is so important to many businesses that special people are hired to provide this information.

The weatherman, as he is called, is really a specially trained scientist in meteorology.

Meteorology is the science of

weather, and the men who study it are called meteorologists.

Meteorologists work for airlines, public utilities, transportation companies, department stores, and the United States Weather Bureau.

No, they do not use a crystal ball. Instead, weather reports from all over the world are studied to determine what kind of weather is moving toward us. The meteorologist uses many instruments to help him in his work.

These instruments tell him the temperature, air pressure, speed and direction of the wind, the amount of moisture in the air—that is, the humidity—the kind of clouds in the sky, the amount of rainfall, and other important information.

Not only does the meteorologist want to know these facts about the air near him, but he also wants the same information about the upper air.

Data about the air fifteen or more miles above the ground is obtained by sending up a large helium-filled plastic balloon. Attached to the balloon is an instrument called a radiosonde. It also contains other instruments. The radiosonde parachutes to earth, and the information is collected.

Here are some instruments used by the weatherman. Some of these end in "meter," a Greek word meaning "measure." You can make some of these for your home or classroom.

THERMOMETER . . . . . measures temperature.
BAROMETER . . . . measures pressure.
ANEMOMETER . . . . . measures speed of wind.
WIND VANE . . . . . indicates direction of wind.
HYGROMETER . . . . measures humidity.
RAIN GAUGE . . . . measures amount of rainfall.

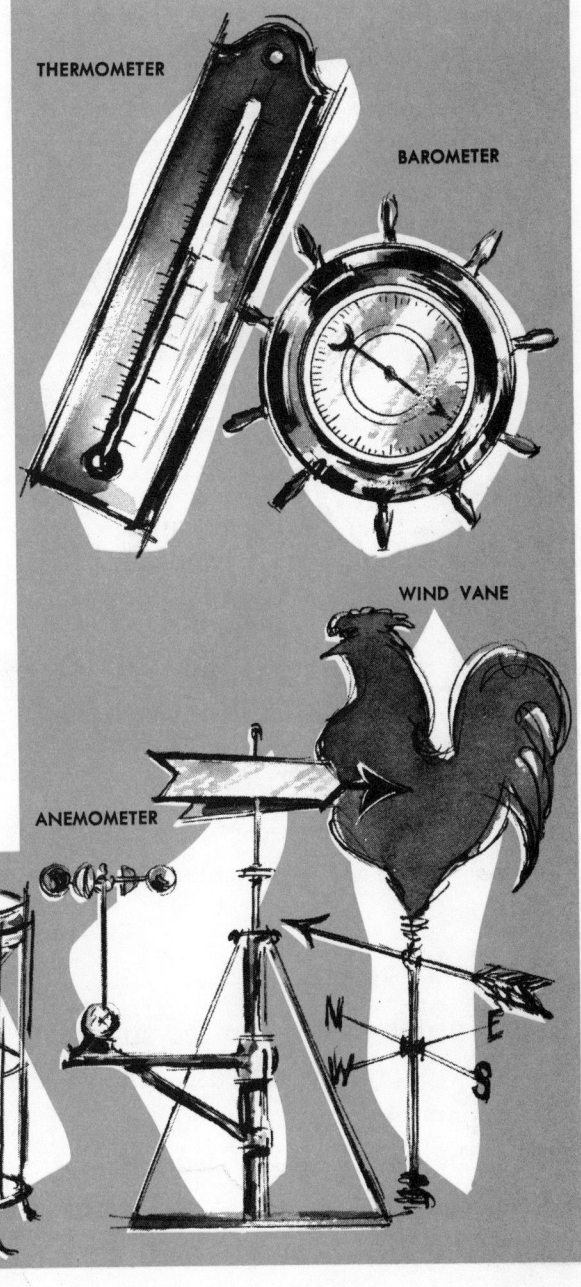

THERMOMETER

BAROMETER

WIND VANE

ANEMOMETER

HYGROMETER

RAIN GAUGE

How Can You Make a Thermometer?

You will use:

Milk bottle with cap
Plastic straw
Wax
Colored water
White card

Do this:

Fill the bottle with colored water.

Place the plastic straw in a hole in the center of the milk-bottle cap.

Melt a little bit of the wax around the straw and around the edge of the cap.

Place a white card behind the straw so that its water level can be easily seen.

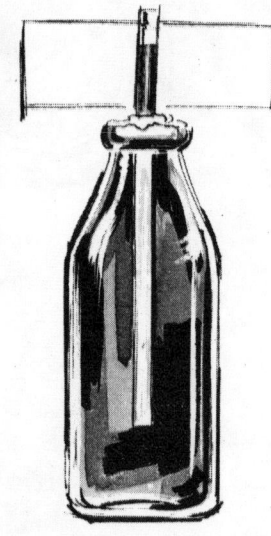

Water will expand and rise as air temperature rises.

What will happen?

The water will rise in the straw. As the air temperature increases, the water will expand and rise even higher.

As the temperature decreases, the water will contract, and the level in the straw will come down.

Here is your chance to be really scientific

Write temperature degrees on the white card and put a commercial thermometer right beside your homemade one. Compare them.

Try to see if it is warmer or cooler near the ceiling by placing the thermometer on a high shelf and then on the floor.

Compare your thermometer with a commercial one.

Does a fan blowing on your thermometer affect it?

Cover it with a dark-colored cloth, and take a reading after a while.

Repeat with a light-colored cloth.

Do you notice any difference?

The cool air from a fan will lower the temperature.

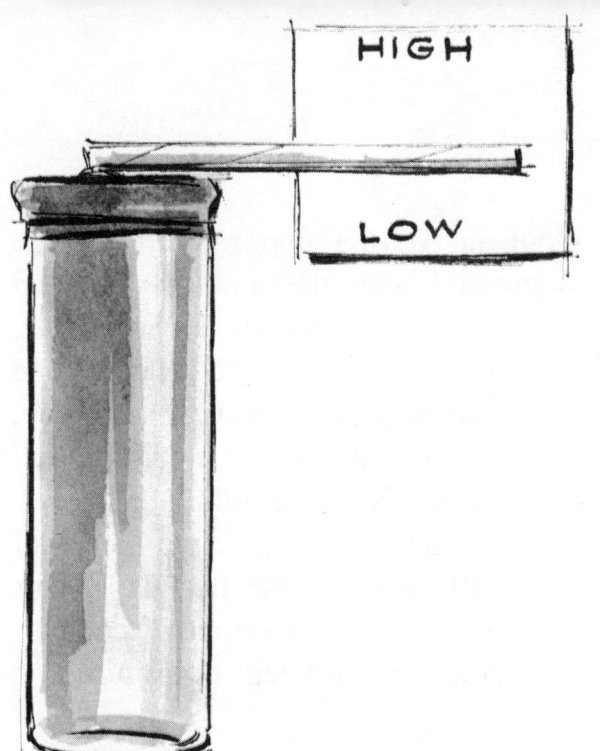

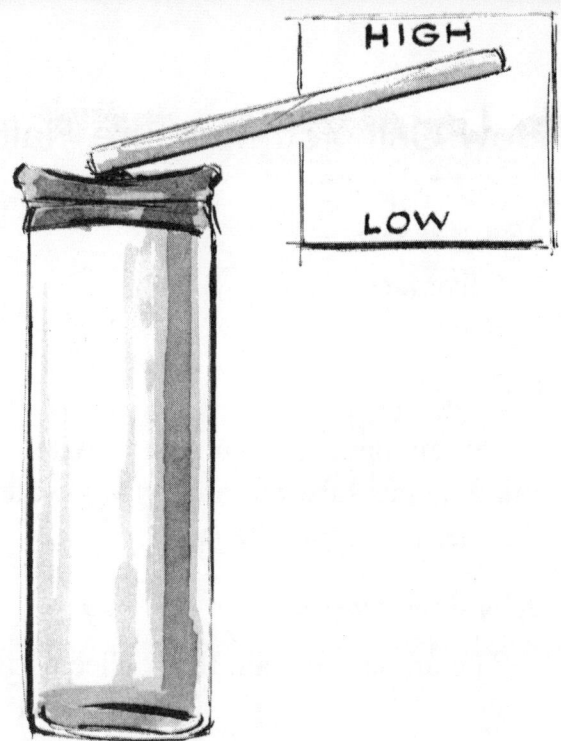

How Can You Test Air Pressure?

You will use:

Olive jar
Rubber balloon
Rubber band
Drinking straw
Glue
White card

Do this:

Cut the balloon so that it can be stretched over the mouth of the jar.

Place the rubber band about the neck of the jar so that the stretched balloon will stay put.

Now place a drop of glue in the center of the piece of balloon.

Place one end of the straw on the glue. Hold it in place until the glue dries.

Place a white card behind the end of the straw.

You have made a barometer.

What will happen?

As the pressure of the air increases, it presses hard in all directions. It presses hard on the jar, on the desk— all over. It also presses on the surface of the balloon, pushing it downward. The end of the straw attached to the balloon dips down, causing the other end to point upward.

This indicates high pressure.

When the air pressure is low, it does not press so hard on objects. In fact, the normal pressure inside the bottle has more force pushing up than the pressure from the outside pushing downward. The result is that the balloon bulges up, causing the far end of the straw to dip down.

This indicates low pressure.

A rapid drop of pressure usually is an indication that bad weather is coming.

Your next project will be to make a rain gauge. It is another instrument that will help you to know more about the weather.

27

How Can You Measure Rain in Inches?

You will use:

Olive jar
Ruler

Do this:

Set an olive jar outdoors. After a rainfall, measure the amount of water that has fallen into the jar.

Why does it work?

The amount of rain that collected in your jar during one rainfall can be compared with the amount recorded during another rainfall. For example, if two inches of water are collected one day and one inch the following day, we can say that twice as much rain fell the first day as the second.

We cannot say that three inches of rain fell during those two days. Our gauge is useful as a means of comparing rainfall on different occasions.

How Can You Tell Which Way the Wind Is Blowing?

You will use:

Cardboard
Pair of scissors
Pin
Pencil with eraser

Do this:

Take a piece of cardboard. Cut out an arrow shaped as follows:

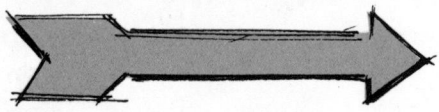

Insert a straight pin through the arrow. Push it through the eraser end of an ordinary pencil.

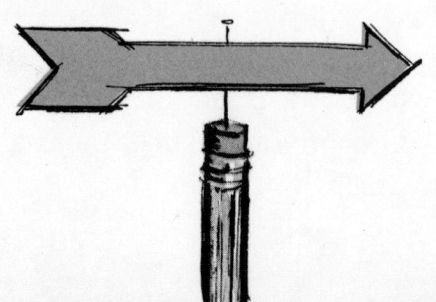

You have made a wind vane.

Take it outdoors. The arrow will turn around in the wind.

What will happen?

The arrow points into the wind. That is, if the arrow points to the north, the wind is coming from the north— it is a north wind.

Set up a real weather bureau, with thermometers, barometers, and a rain gauge to measure the amount of rainfall.

Don't forget the weather maps. The meteorologist uses these maps to find out about weather conditions in other localities, states, and even other countries.

Here are some symbols (used on these weather maps) you should know. They help us learn about the weather, as reported to Washington, D.C., by our country's approximately 300 observing stations. Local stations also send their reports to eight major weather stations located in New York City, Atlanta, Kansas City, Chicago, Los Angeles, Fort Worth, Seattle, and Anchorage, Alaska.

Some of the symbols you should be familiar with are seen below.

The future in weather forecasting is a very bright one.

On April 1, 1960, the United States launched Tiros I, a 270-pound satellite which sent back to earth TV pictures of numerous clouds and storms. The United States Weather Bureau has indicated that meteorological satellite development offers promise of one of the most revolutionary advances in the history of the science of meteorology.

Perhaps some day you will be able to plan a picnic weeks in advance, safe in the knowledge that the weatherman has forecast a sunny day.

Weather bureaus all over the country use certain symbols on their charts to indicate the daily weather picture.

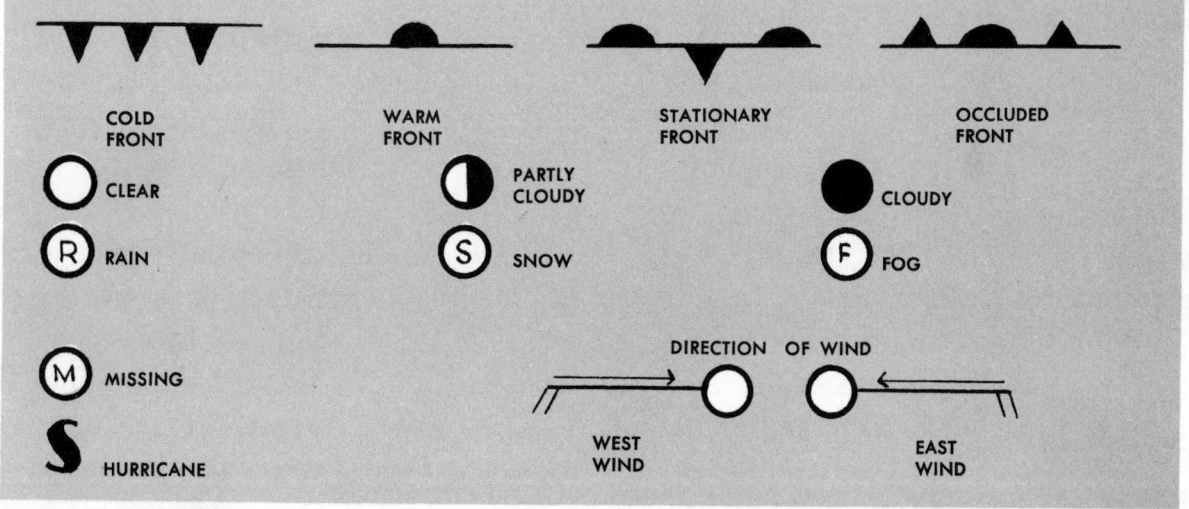

COLD FRONT   WARM FRONT   STATIONARY FRONT   OCCLUDED FRONT

O CLEAR   ◑ PARTLY CLOUDY   ● CLOUDY

Ⓡ RAIN   Ⓢ SNOW   Ⓕ FOG

Ⓜ MISSING

𝐒 HURRICANE

DIRECTION OF WIND

WEST WIND   EAST WIND

Transportation — "Let's Go!"

Important Words

Friction: Resistance to motion caused by the rubbing of one surface against another surface.

Internal Combustion: In an internal combustion engine, such as is found in an automobile, fuel and air mix and explode within the cylinders to cause parts to move.

Jet Propulsion: The force of expanding air or gases rushing out of a rear opening causes an object, such as a rocket or a plane, to move forward.

Steam: Vapor from boiling water. It can be used to make many things move.

In ancient times—and even in some places on earth today—carrying or pushing was man's only means of transporting heavy burdens from one place to another. Later these burdens were placed on animals—oxen, donkeys and horses. In fact, less than a century ago, American Indians carried their goods on travois pulled by horses.

The wheel changed all this. At first, man had a crude, heavy wheel. After many refinements, he developed the wagon wheel and then the automobile wheel, which today moves along highways with speed, safety, and comfort.

How do you think the Egyptians were able to build those huge pyramids without powerful engines to operate cranes?

They used their muscles and their intelligence. We know that the Egyptians had a wheel. It was covered with leather which was secured to the wheel by means of rawhide strips.

Later on, the Greeks and Romans developed better and more decorative wheels for their chariots.

Let's do an experiment to show how rolling helps us move things.

"Let's go" is a common expression meaning to say, "Let's travel," "Let's sail," "Let's fly," or "Let's transport something." Not so long ago it often meant getting around by horse and buggy—if the weather wasn't too bad and, more important, if the roads were in good shape.

Our modern way of life has not only changed the means of transportation, but it has also made it possible to travel easily to distant places and to transport enormous weights by rail, ship and air.

Why Do Wheels Make Work Easier?

You will use:

Shoebox
Three round pencils
String
Several books
Spring scale

Do this:

Attach the string to the box so that you can pull it. Place several books inside the box.

Attach the spring scale to the string. Pull the box.

How much did the scale measure? Write it down.

Place three round pencils under the box. Pull the box.

How much did the scale measure? Compare your results.

Which rolled easier? Why?

Why it works:

Round objects, such as rollers and wheels, make moving easier than pulling flat objects. This is because there is less friction between a round object and the surface it is rolling on.

Wheels offer even less resistance than rollers.

Let's see if we can begin to understand how jet planes work.

Round objects reduce friction and make the movement of heavy articles easier.

How Do Jet Planes Work?

You will use:

Plastic boat
Medicine dropper
Balloon
Rubber band

Do this:

Remove the rubber part of the medicine dropper.

Place the wide end of the glass medicine dropper about 1 inch into the neck of the balloon. Secure it firmly with a rubber band.

Place a balloon in a toy rowboat. The principle of jet propulsion can be demonstrated in a bathtub of water.

Carefully punch a hole in the rear of the boat. Insert the dropper so that it emerges outside the boat.

Place some water in a bathtub.

Blow up the balloon through the medicine dropper. Hold your finger over the opening, and place the boat in the tub. What happens?

Now take your finger off the opening. In which direction does the boat go?

Why it works:

The air inside a closed balloon pushes evenly in all directions. Therefore, the balloon is not forced to move in any direction.

When the balloon is opened, air rushes out the opening. Since the pressure at this end is being reduced, the pressure at the opposite end causes the balloon to move in that direction. Therefore, as the air escapes to the rear, the balloon and the boat move forward through the water.

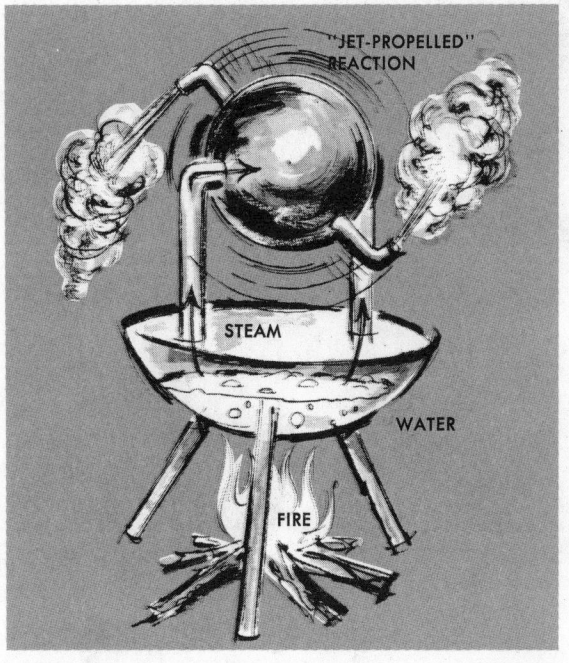

Hero of Alexandria, a Greek scientist who lived about 2,000 years ago, was the first man to demonstrate the principle of jet propulsion. He built a kind of engine as shown above. Fire boiled the water which sent steam through two pipes connected to a hollow ball. Two smaller pipes attached to the ball released the steam, propelling the hollow sphere.

People often ask, "Is jet power something new?" It isn't.

For example, we know that Hero, a

The action of a jet plane can be shown in this experiment which you can make with a balloon. Blow up a balloon. Then release it. A fast stream of air rushes from the neck of the balloon. But the balloon will move in the opposite direction of the stream of air.

Greek mathematician and writer who lived in Alexandria, Egypt, about 150 B.C., demonstrated jet action with steam.

First of all, when water boils—or, as scientists say, reaches the boiling point of 212 degrees Fahrenheit—it begins to change into steam—that is, the molecules of water get energy from the heat source and begin to spread out. They move in all directions, especially out. These tiny molecules of water, having gotten a lot of pep and vigor from the heat, really push hard to escape. It's this push that makes them into the vapor we call steam.

Have you ever listened to a whistling teakettle? It's the steam that blows the whistle.

When steam is put under pressure, it can do a lot of work. Scientists have even measured how much steam we can get from a certain amount of water. For example, one cubic inch of water, when heated to the boiling point, makes about one cubic foot of steam.

How would you like to make a simple steam turbine and see exactly how it works?

How Does a Steam Engine Work?

You will use:

Empty coffee can
4 by 4 inch piece of aluminum foil
Pin
Cork
Hammer
Thin nail
Pencil with eraser
Scissors

Do this:

Hammer the nail into the cover of the can, about 1 inch from the edge, to make a hole.

Make a pinwheel from the aluminum foil. Cut each corner to about ½ inch of the center.

Pin every other corner through the center.

Place the pin through the eraser of your pencil.

Test your pinwheel by blowing on it or by waving it through the air.

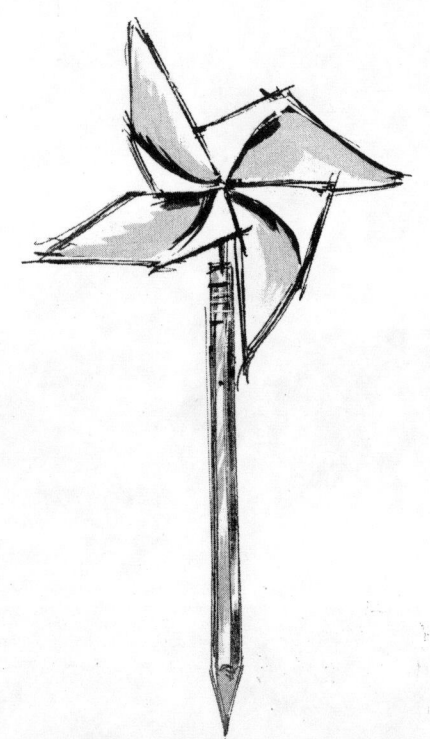

Press the sharpened end of the pencil into the side of the cork.

Nail or glue the cork to the center of the coffee-can cover, so that the blades of the pinwheel are above the hole in the cover.

Put a little water in the can. Put on the cover, and place the can on the range.

Soon the pinwheel will begin to spin.

Why it works:

When the water begins to boil, it changes into steam and rushes through the small opening at the top of the can.

The force of the steam pushes against the blades of the pinwheel and turns it.

On a large scale, the steam can do much more work. The more heat applied, the more steam we get.

The steam engine replaced lesser sources of energy, and people began moving about more.

Robert Fulton used steam to enable

35

ships to travel under their own power. No longer did ships have to depend upon favorable winds to give them power. Burning wood or coal produced the steam to send the ships on their way.

If steam power was such a terrific advance, you may imagine how important the invention of the gasoline engine was.

Ask your Dad to open the hood of

Without the steam engine (cutaway, left), we would have had to rely on the wind to move ships, and horses to pull our trains during those early days.

Later on, the invention of the gasoline engine, or internal combustion machine, greatly increased our transportation possibilities, making travel easier and faster. The use of atomic power will further these possibilities.

his car and let you look inside. The gasoline engine of an automobile works on the principle of internal combustion —that is, explosions take place inside cylinders in the engine block. Each explosion is caused when gasoline vapor mixed with air is ignited by a spark from the spark plug.

The explosion forces the piston inside the cylinder to go down and turn the crankshaft.

We hope that now you are beginning to understand what an internal combustion engine is.

We also hope that you are beginning to understand what is meant when people say that the world has become smaller. Today we can get from one place to another much faster and with much less trouble than people were ever able to do in the past.

Imagine how much easier it will be to travel when atomic power is used in planes, trains, and even automobiles.

The Vegetable Kingdom — Plants

Important Words

Chlorophyll: The green coloring of plants.

Erosion: The wearing-away of the land.

Photosynthesis: The process used by green plants to manufacture their own food.

Pollen: Yellow dust produced by stamens. The pollen helps form new seeds in the plants.

Stomata: Tiny openings in the leaf of a plant, through which oxygen and carbon dioxide pass.

Someone once said that without plants it would be impossible for anything to live on earth.

Let's trace the history of a hamburger or a steak to find out if that's true. It comes from a steer. The steer cannot exist without grass—a plant. What about bread? It is made from a plant —wheat. What about eggs? They come from an animal that depends upon plants for food. What about sugar? That was originally from a plant. Honey would not be made if bees could not get pollen from plants. We could trace back any food this way. It all comes down to this: No plants—no life.

Let's begin by finding out how a plant takes care of itself by manufacturing its own food in its own factory. We know that an animal has to be fed.

Someone must give it food or else it roams around in search of it. We humans have our food prepared for us. It is not so with plants.

Did you ever see how a furniture factory operates? For one thing, you see trucks carrying raw materials— such as planks of lumber, cans of varnish and paint, and kegs of nails— which get unloaded on the platforms. Then you see other trucks carrying finished products—such as chairs and tables—neatly packed and ready for sale, pulling away from the loading platforms of the factory.

The plant factory does not have trucks delivering its raw materials. These materials are carbon dioxide, water, and sunlight. Once the plant has these materials, it goes into operation. The leaf of the plant takes in two of these raw materials—carbon dioxide and sunlight—while water is taken in through the roots. The leaf has tiny openings called stomata. If you look at a section of a leaf under a microscope, you can see these openings.

Leaves "inhale" carbon dioxide and "exhale" oxygen through small holes called stomata (enlarged).

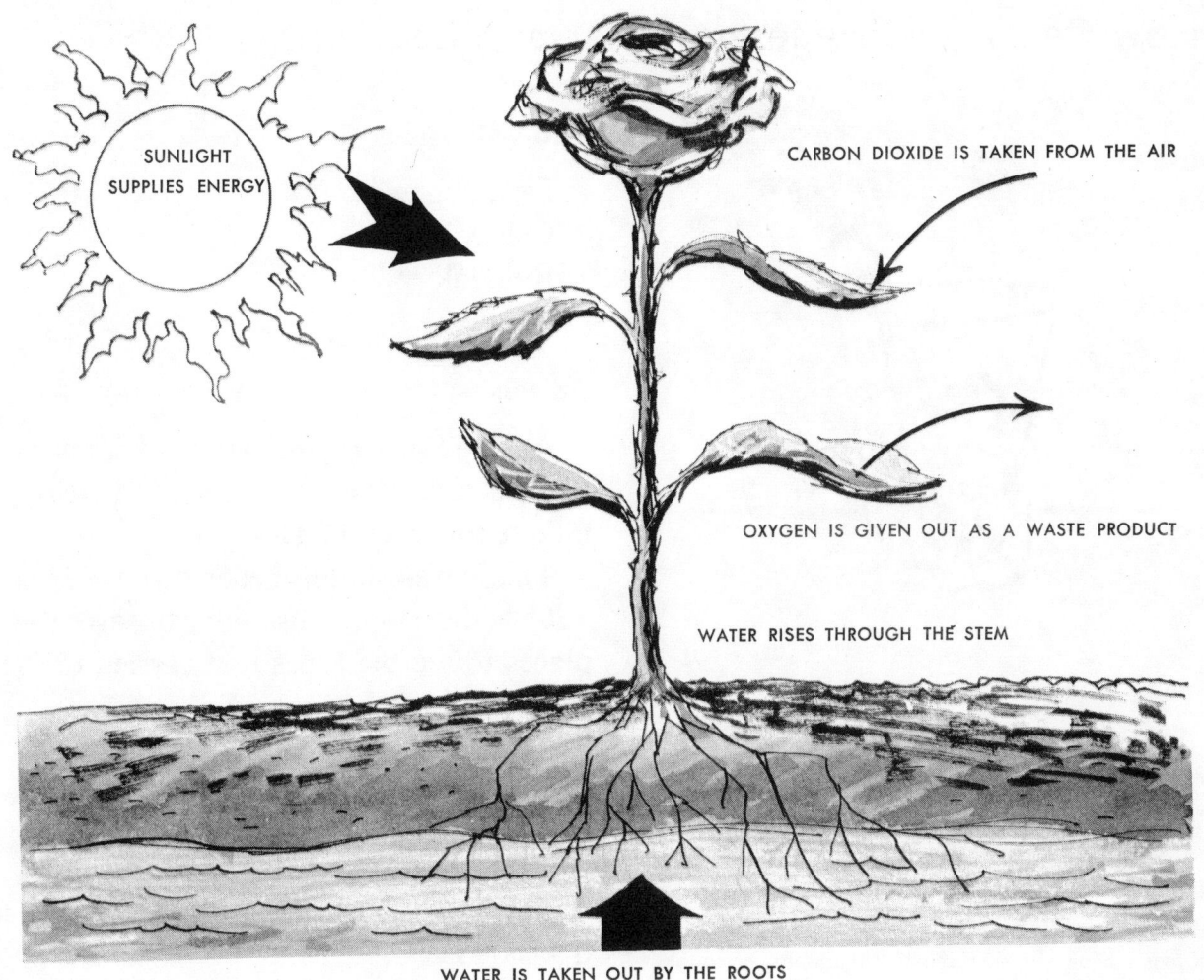

SUNLIGHT SUPPLIES ENERGY

CARBON DIOXIDE IS TAKEN FROM THE AIR

OXYGEN IS GIVEN OUT AS A WASTE PRODUCT

WATER RISES THROUGH THE STEM

WATER IS TAKEN OUT BY THE ROOTS

After the openings take in the raw materials, chemical changes take place. The raw materials—carbon dioxide, water, and sun—go to work on the tiny bits of matter inside the leaf. These bits of matter give the plant its green color and are called chlorophyll. The result of this work is the manufacture of sugar. In the process, oxygen is given off.

The sugar is used in all parts of the plant to help it live and grow.

This making of food has a name we should know. It is called photosynthesis.

That is quite a word. What does it mean? Let's take the word apart and see. You've heard of "photo"—it means "light." "Synthesis" means "building up" or "putting together." The whole word means "putting together under the influence of light."

Plants don't depend upon their leaves for water. Instead, they get water from the earth through a special tube system of roots and root hairs. Roots do more than get moisture and minerals for the food-making of a plant. In addition, they serve as anchors. Like a ship, they have to be anchored so that they don't drift off as a result of wind and rain. The roots hold the soil together and prevent what we call erosion, or the wearing away of the soil.

How Can You Change the Color of a Leaf?

You will use:

Drinking glass
Celery stalk
Red ink
Water

Do this:

Add red ink to a half-glass of water. Place a celery stalk in the glass. Leave it there for several hours.

The leaves should become red.

Cut the stem crosswise in several places to see the tubes that carried the water to the leaves.

Why it works:

Cross section of a stem showing the tubes, or canals.

The stems carry the water to the leaves by means of small tubes or pipes. Water rises like an elevator to reach the leaves.

A more interesting experiment can be made in which a white flower is given two different colors. Split the stalk of a white flower in half and place each end of the stalk in a separate glass of water, each of a different color. After some time has elapsed, you will notice that one half of the flower is of one color, and the other half is of another color. To vary the experiment, it is also possible to cut the stalk in three sections or even in quarters.

Do Green Plants Need Sunlight?

You will use:

Two similar potted plants
One large box to serve as a cover

Do this:

Cover one plant with the large box.
Make several holes in the box to let
air in.

Water both plants daily.

What will happen?

After several days, compare the
healthy, green, uncovered plant with
the one that was covered.

The covered plant will probably be
yellowed and frail.

Sunlight was kept from the plant.
It did not have the opportunity to manufacture its own food. The plant suffered
from "malnutrition."

Try to revive the plant by placing it
in the sun.

Do Plants Bend Toward the Sun?

You will use:

Green plant
Large corrugated box

Do this:

Make an opening in the side of the box at about the height the leaves will reach when placed inside.

Place the plant in the box. Have the opening of the box directly in the path of the sun.

What will happen?

After several days the leaves and stems are bent toward the light of the sun.

Turn the plant so the leaves point away from the opening. After several more days they will again turn toward the light.

Again we see that green plants need sunlight and grow toward it.

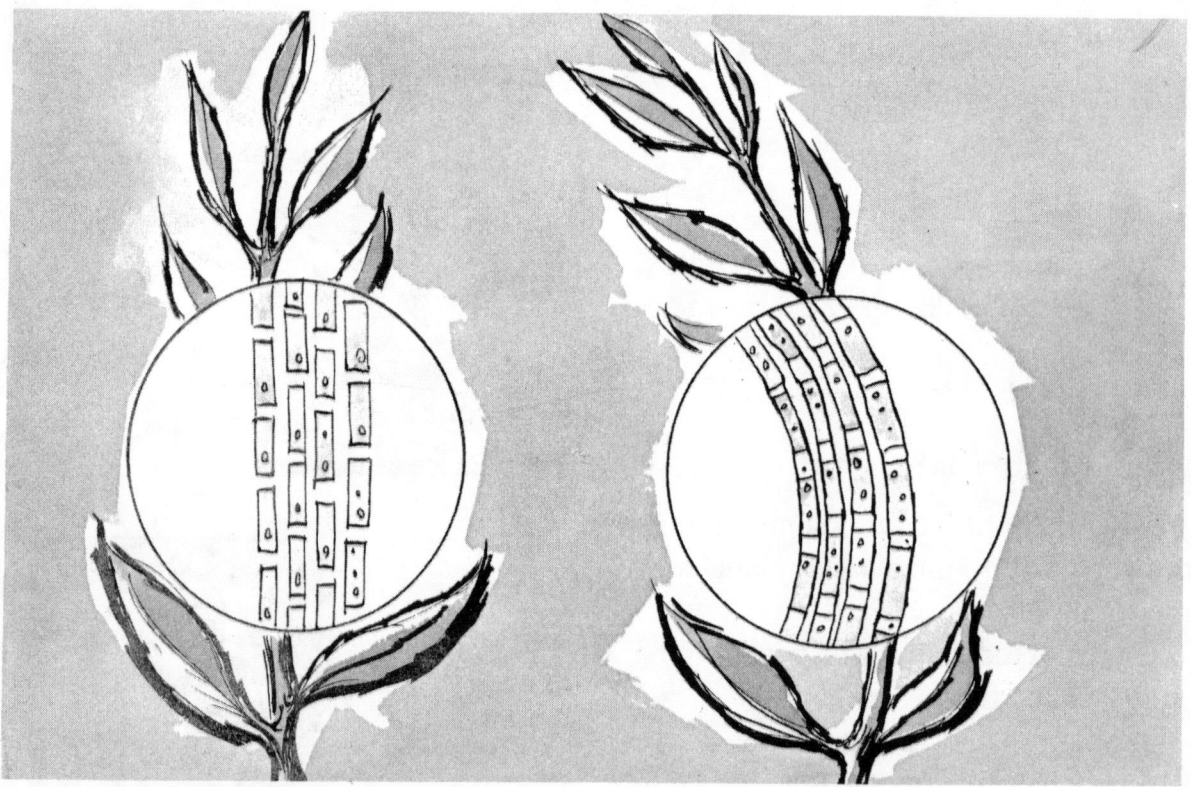

When a plant is growing straight up, an examination of its cells would show that they were about uniform in size. However, when the plant cells on one side grow larger than the cells on the other side, the plant will bend.

Do Green Plants Need Water?

You will use:

Two similar potted plants

Do this:

Place both flowerpots in the sunlight.
Water one plant daily. Do not water the other.
Label each pot accordingly.

What will happen?

After several days, notice that one plant is thriving while the other is wilted and dying.

Water, which is necessary for photosynthesis, was kept from one plant. The plant was unable to manufacture its food and began to die.

Try to revive it by watering it.

A plant that has enough water grows.

Without enough water a plant will wither.

Do Green Plants Need Air?

You will use:

Two similar potted plants
Large jar
Two small dishes of water

Do this:

Place each flowerpot in a small dish of water.
Cover one plant with a jar.
Press the jar into the soil so that no air can reach the plant.
Place both plants in sunlight.

What will happen?

Observe what happens after several days.

The plant getting the air will show great vitality and life.

We have seen so far that plants need light, water, and air.

All plants "breathe." Without air they would die.

FLOATING

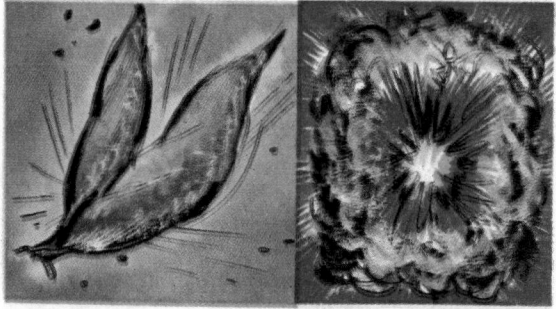

EXPLODING

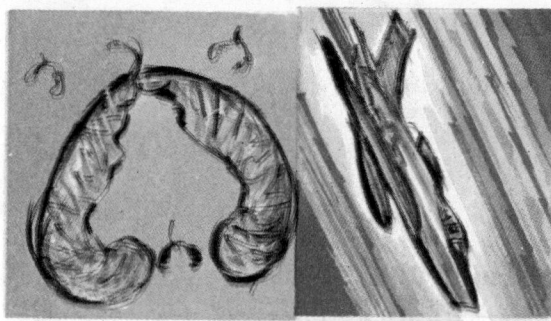

FLYING

STICKING

HITCHHIKING

So far, we have only been considering half the story. We have learned about leaves and roots but not about flowers and stems.

Do you remember why we said that leaves and roots are important? Leaves help the plant make food for itself. And roots and root hairs help to bring moisture and minerals to feed the plant.

Now, the flower's job is to help the plant produce more plants. Here's how it happens.

Look at this tulip. Those flat lollipop-shaped objects inside the petals are called stamens. Squeeze the tip. Do you see the yellow powder? That's called pollen. When an insect visits a flower, some of the pollen sticks to its body and legs. This pollen drops off as the insect goes to another flower. Sometimes wind blows pollen from flower to flower. If the pollen falls on this sticky, vase-shaped part of the flower, called the pistil, it grows down the pistil to form seeds. When the seeds ripen, they may grow into new plants.

Look at the seeds the next time you eat an apple. If you throw the core into the garden, do you think an apple tree will grow?

It might. Some plants have interesting ways of scattering seeds that parachute to earth. Others are exploded into the air. Some fly or glide. There are seeds that stick to animals and still others that are scattered by birds.

You may not have realized that a plant is so complicated. And we haven't

Seeds, almost like the actions of men, it seems, can float, explode, fly in the air, stick, and are carried away. These are the ways seeds are scattered about.

A TYPICAL GREEN PLANT

Cross section through a flower

mentioned another use for seeds. We eat seeds. Think of stringbeans and peas. Rice is a most wonderful seed. A great part of the population of the world eats rice as its main food. We eat wheat, corn, barley, cereals—like oats. Why, we even get oils from seeds —from corn, cotton, peanuts and sunflowers.

We also eat the leaves of plants, such as lettuce and cabbage. And when we eat cauliflower, we're eating the flower of the plant. And we also eat stems, such as asparagus and celery.

We also benefit from other parts of plants and trees. We get paper from wood pulp, as well as wood for toys, furniture and houses.

The sap of a tree is also important. You know the syrup your mother serves with wheatcakes for breakfast? Yes, that's part of the sap of a tree.

Here's a problem. The automobile would never be as popular as it is today if it were not for the sap of a tree. Can you tell why?

The answer is that the sap of some trees gives the raw rubber for our tires.

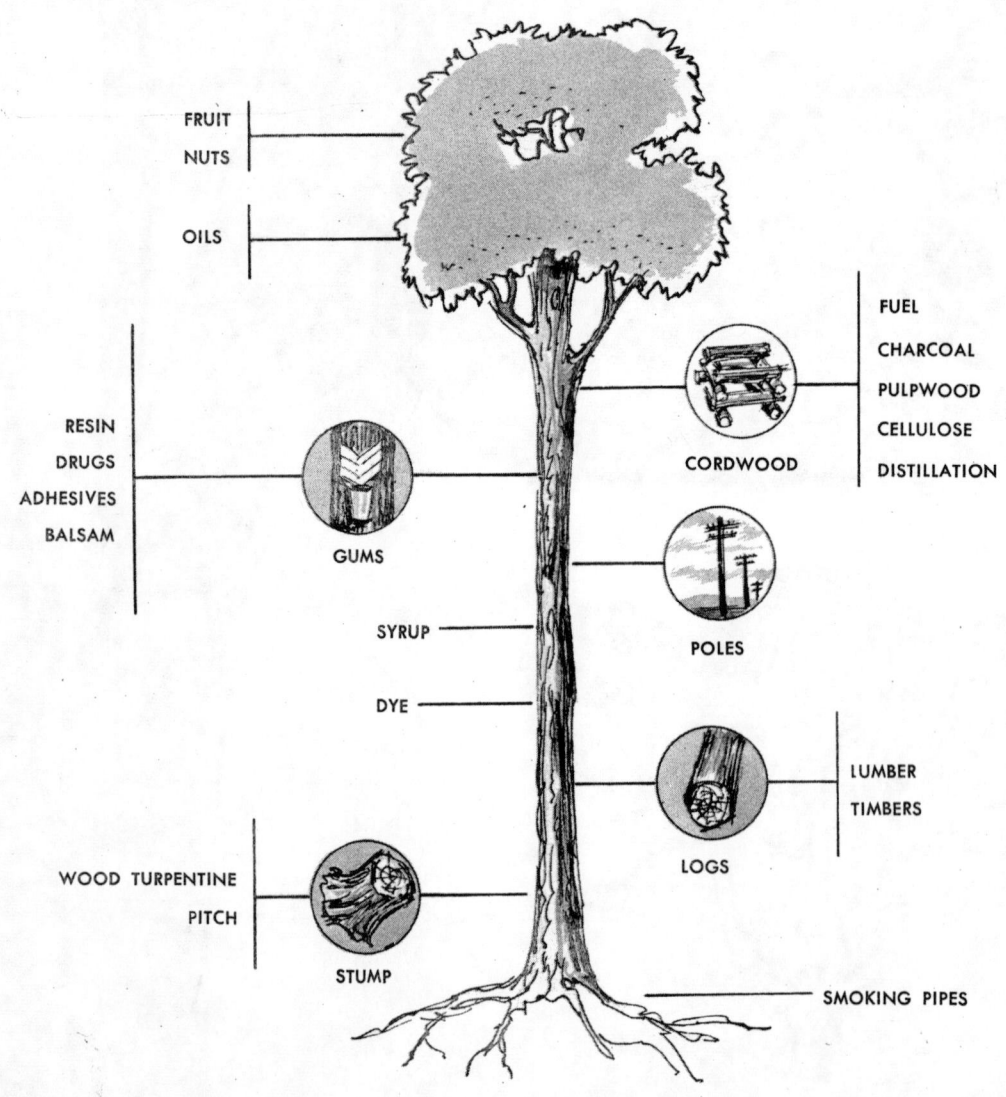

The bark, sap, roots and foliage of trees have given man several useful products for home and industry.

Can You See Seeds Grow?

You will use:

Olive jar
Absorbent cotton
Seeds, such as pumpkin, lima bean, corn, pea

Do this:

Fill the olive jar with cotton.
Place seeds between the cotton and the glass.
Do not place seeds too close to each other.
Wet the cotton and keep it damp for several days.

What will happen?

After several days the shoots or stems will be growing upward and the roots will be growing downward.

Invert the glass.

After several more days the stems and roots will turn so that again the stems grow up and the roots grow down.

If the seeds continue growing in the glass for several days, you will notice that they appear to be dying. Why do you think this happens? The plants seem to be getting everything they need for photosynthesis—carbon dioxide, water, and sunlight. But they are missing some minerals that are found in soil. Up to this point, each plant was living off itself. It was getting its nourishment from the food stored in the seed. Now that it is ready to manufacture its own food, it should have these minerals.

You can revive the plants by placing them in flowerpots with soil.

The shoots grow upward and the roots downward.

Inverted glass: Shoots still grow up, roots down.

Some Famous Men of Science

Luther Burbank (1849-1926), American, plant scientist who developed many new varieties of plant.

George Washington Carver (1864-1943), American, botanist and chemist who found many uses for peanuts, sweet potatoes, and soybeans.

Thomas Alva Edison (1847-1931), American, inventor of the electric light bulb.

Michael Faraday (1791-1867), English, made the first electric generator.

Henry Ford (1863-1947), American, pioneer in the development of the automobile and its manufacture.

Robert Fulton (1765-1815), American, inventor of the first commercially successful steamboat.

James Clerk-Maxwell (1831-1879), Scot, formulated theories of light.

Albert Abraham Michelson (1852-1931), American, determined the speed of light.

Isaac Newton (1642-1727), English, scientist and philosopher; among his many achievements was his work in the field of light.

Max Planck (1858-1947), German, Nobel Prize winner for his theory of light.

Charles Proteus Steinmetz (1865-1923), American, made many contributions in the field of electrical engineering.

Evangelista Torricelli (1608-1647), Italian, invented the barometer.

Alessandro Volta (1745-1827), Italian, made the first cell that produced an electric current.

Orville Wright (1871-1948) and Wilbur Wright (1867-1912), American, pioneers in the invention and development of the airplane.